The Front

Dental Office Lessons

Management • Marketing • Miscellaneous

By M.M. Bateman

ISBN: 1490925619
ISBN-13: 9781490925615

Dedication

Dedicated to my husband and best friend,
Rick and our two awesome sons,
Kenan and Davis.

Introduction

Ever have one of those days? The lab messes up a case and the patient blames you. The office staff is arguing and not being team players. The patient wants you to pay for a mistake in insurance estimation. A patient complains that his hygienist was too rough even though he has raging periodontal disease. Payroll is due and you do not have the collections to pay your staff so you have to borrow money from your equity account. You are late for an important lunch because a patient was late for their appointment and you needed that production to pay the bills.

Does it all go bad at the same time? It is out of control and you want out. It seems so much easier to just chuck it and work for someone else who can worry about running a business.

What if you found solutions to running the business so you can enjoy being in charge and doing what you love? Running a business can be fun and rewarding (and lucrative) as long as you take control of a few aspects of the day-to-day tasks. If you want to charge ahead, find energy to run the business and do what you like to do, read on. I have put together ideas and suggestions about how to run your business efficiently so you can delegate, control and love your career.

Dental and medical businesses are just that, a *business.*

Healthcare is just like any other business. Owners, clinical staff and business staff are trained professionals and deserve to make money and not work for free. Although many feel differently, the business and profitability of healthcare has to exist or these talented healthcare providers cannot pay their rent/mortgage, buy their food, pay off their educational loans or buy their gas to get to work. If you feel dental and medical should be non-profit then hats off to you, there is a place for that. However, this book focuses on helping small dental and medical practices work smoother, faster, more efficiently and produce a better bottom line.

Management

The Business Office - Called the Front Desk

Sometimes the business office staff is referred to as the "Front Desk". These staff members are not a piece of furniture so call them either the Business Office or the Front. "The Front Desk" sounds like the business office staff members are an afterthought or not very important. What you will find is that the business staff is very important in retaining patients, signing new patients and filling your calendar. It is important to respect this staff just as you do the clinical staff.

Many times the business office has very little interaction with the doctor so they are an afterthought in patient care and interaction. All the "business stuff" just happens and doctors do not want to get involved for the most part. They really do not hear the interaction with patients like they observe first hand with clinical staff members. So, with some of the guidelines this book provides, the doctor will see what he or she needs to put into place to "professionalize" the business office so they obtain the respect they deserve. Let's look into their roles and embrace how important it is for the practice to obtain, retain and schedule patients.

The Business Office - Professional Appearance

Hopefully all the clinical staff provides a clean, orderly area for patients. Take a look. Are all operatories organized, clean, and maintained? Does the clinical staff have matching scrubs or smocks with their name embroidered? Do they all follow the same procedure? More than likely these details are already in place. Patients notice details.

When it comes to your business office, the same details need to be followed. Take a test drive through the practice as if you are a new patient. Park and walk in the front door. Pretend you are a patient who has never been in your office and critique your office with fresh eyes.

Is the parking lot clean of debris? Are the parking spaces clearly striped and signage clean and easy to read? Is the front door clean, does it squeak, is the handle nice and easy to grip? The front door is the first thing that is touched by the patient. It must be very nice and tell a story about your practice. If you have a lot of stickers or advertisements, that means you are heavy into marketing. If the handle is loose or old or lightweight, it sends a message that you are not up to date. You would be surprised how that very first impression goes a long way.

When you sit in the waiting room, how does it look? Check the carpet for stains or worn areas. Sit in the seats. Pay attention to what you hear coming from the inside of the office. Patients can hear staff members talking so notice how voices travel. Your staff may need to talk softer and the staff should never discuss patients where the conversation can be overheard. Walk through the rest of the patient spaces to get an idea of how to improve the patient experience.

When it comes to the actual business office personnel, appearance is very important. I have seen dentists and doctors who perform mostly cosmetic procedures try to hire only the best looking staff they can find to represent the business office without regard to any skills. That is fine if that is the message you are trying to convey, however when it comes to dentists and doctors who are trying to do cosmetic **and** other procedures, it is important to have the business office look professional. It is important to hire staff that has a nice smile; even if you have to fix their teeth after they are hired.

Your business office should appear like professional businesspeople because that sends a message to patients that your business staff can be taken seriously and they are not just order takers. I recommend the staff dress in professional shirts and slacks. Nametags or embroidered shirts are a good idea. Even if you just embroider the name of the practice, that is fine but I recommend putting their name somewhere so patients know to whom they are talking.

Please do not have the business office dress in scrubs. The business office is not going to dash to the back and do a quick crown prep so scrubs are not appropriate. Business office personnel are not clinical and should not portray that appearance. You do not want what they say to be perceived as a clinical opinion. There are liability issues with this. So, please ask them to dress as though they work in a bank. They are running your business and need to be perceived as business professionals. Dressing alike is great and necessary. Many times the front business office likes to coordinate colors for certain days and it looks very professional and it conveys a team atmosphere. I really like it when the staff coordinates their color of shirt. Do not allow low cut blouses, short skirts, or tight fitting clothes.

It is important to keep the business office clean and clutter free. The less paper the better. Patients like to see that their chart and their personal information is protected so leaving information out for others to see is a no-no. Keep any items you need to use in folders so you can easily close the folder if a patient walks up.

Also, the dreaded Post it notes need to be put away. Some staff members like to have reminders around their computers so they leave up Post it notes to remind them. This is not helpful because if you get used to a note that has been posted for a while, you will not see it as new so it did not remind you anyway. Strip all sticky notes and place them inside a desk drawer or in a daily folder that your staff checks when they start their day. Or better yet, place a reminder in the computer so your staff will not forget the issue and patients cannot see it. Many of the new dental software companies have great pop-up reminders. Other software suites such as ACT!, Evernote and others are easy to use.

Here's an example of the problems with Post-It Notes. One office had a note up for the treatment coordinator about monthly billing. It listed patients who did not get interest charges because they were paying monthly for their dental work. A patient walked up to check out one day and saw their neighbor on that list. They told that neighbor about their name being "displayed". The neighbor moved their business elsewhere because privileged information had been leaked, and the client who saw the note moved their business elsewhere because of shoddy privacy practices. Because of one note, the practice lost business from two families. No one can afford that too often, so strip away the notes and put them in files or on computer where no one can access them except your staff.

Hiring and Firing

There's an old saying that goes "hire slow - fire fast." Hiring slowly and methodically is a good practice. "Hiring slow" means to interview many times, have (paid) trial days, check all references and backgrounds. Take your time because this professional is the representative of your business so the staff answering phones and interacting with patients is your most important hire. Hire the friendliest business office staff you can find. They must have a great attitude, be quick to laugh, and not take things personally. You can't teach friendly; everything else can be taught.

Yes, you want your staff to have great dental office experience, but it is more important to have a great practice representative rather than an experienced representative with a bad attitude. The professional who answers the phone must be friendly and helpful so patients want to come into your office. A gruff "order taker" answering phones will not get you new patients. The first person patients speak to is their first impression of your business.

Many times it is best to promote within so hire the friendly representative as your receptionist and as other positions are open, promote her/him.

When hiring, please make sure you document their employment expectations. Write a memo to the employee stating their hire date, first review (within 30 days is appropriate), their salary (and when that will be reviewed), bonus system, benefits and expectations. Have them sign the letter so there is a good understanding about what you expect. If there is a probationary period, include that in the offer letter as well.

Firing is always hard no matter what. However, it is something that every business owner and manager must learn to deal with. If a new employee proves to be a problem within the first 30 days, get rid of them. Document everything along the way and review as often as possible within the first 30 days. Then fire them quickly, no notice and ask them to leave the premises. Check the laws of your state to make sure what documentation and notices are required but for the most part, make it simple and quick.

Thinking things will improve or just hoping you can change the behavior is just avoiding the inevitable confrontation. Dragging out the firing with a working notice or a lot of explanation only hurts you and the (former) employee and can open you up to liability if you say the wrong thing. Consult an attorney or HR professional about the laws in your state or city/town, don't construe anything in this book as legal advice.

Salutations

When greeting patients either by phone or in person, the business office should treat each patient as if they are a guest because *they are*. Each patient is a guest to the practice and should feel as though they are the honored guest of the hour. After all, if not for the patient, the employees and owner would not have a job.

The patient is your CUSTOMER. Do not forget that, ever. They must be respected and given every ounce of your time and respect. They are paying your bills so take good care of each one. Don't forget, no matter where you are located, there is competition. The patient/ customer / client has a choice where to go so remember to treat each one as your golden ticket.

When your staff is greeting a patient as they walk in the door, they should always stand and say hello. If possible, refer to the patient by name.

Have a conversation with every patient. You and your staff will greet them then ask how you can help them. Once they respond, you respond with "great", "I am glad you are here" and the best response is "Great! We are going to take good care of you today." You have to change this up for every patient so it does not sound canned because more than likely there will be someone in the area who you just said that to so come up with several responses that you can use. The most important thing you can say to a patient is that "we care about you" or "we will take good care of you" because you will and you do.

When the assistant or hygienist transitions the patient to the business office, the patient is introduced (again). The business office professional asks them how things went. They really *listen* to what the patient says. The hygienist or assistant explains the treatment the patient received or needs. It is imperative to repeat this again so that the patient has a clear understanding of their past and future dental treatment(s). The business office professional repeats what the hygienist or assistant stated the treatment is or was. If new treatment was prescribed, then they repeat what new treatment needs to be scheduled so the patient hears it again. Many times you will notice that a typical patient does not listen to diagnosis carefully so reiteration is necessary. Three times is the minimum when it comes to repetition. This means the doctor mentions it, the hygienist/assistant repeats it to the front and the front repeats it to the patient.

Here is the most important part of this process: the front office professional asks the patient when is a good time to get their treatment scheduled or suggest a time. DO NOT bring up their financial responsibility at this point because if you are prescribing necessary treatment, the treatment needs to be scheduled. The clinical staff must be honest with the patient that there is necessary work to complete and they must tell the business office what is necessary IN FRONT of the patient. Too many times the scheduler prints out a treatment plan outlining the costs and starts the conversation by explaining how the money works first with little regard to the patient's condition.

It is more important to have treatment discussed first so the patient understands what needs to be done, then schedule the treatment, *then* talk about money matters. Yes, it is important to let the patient know what their insurance can cover or not cover (or if they are self-pay, let them know what the total is). However, if you bring up the economics first, you appear to be focused on money rather than what is important for the patient's health. Emphasize the necessary treatment first then talk about the finances. By talking about the budget first, the practice seems like it is focused on profitability rather than patient care. It is more effective to emphasize treatment because in reality, we are here to provide treatment and take good care of our patients.

The dentist or hygienist should never discuss fees or insurance with the patient while they are in the treatment room. The clinical staff needs to stay in the prescription mode and refer the patient to the front to discuss payment. There needs to be a clear separation of the treatment expense and the importance of the treatment.

Once the patient is scheduled, the front staff then asks them if they would like to go over insurance or how the payment works. That gives the business office a chance to discuss money but at this point, it is upon the patient's request. If the treatment plan is large or over $500, the staff member needs ask them if they can go over options. It is the business office staff's responsibility to review finances with patients. Most patients will guide you into the treatment price conversation. The bottom line is do not bring up money first because it looks like you do not care about the patient's treatment. Bring up their dental investment only after the patient is scheduled.

Also make sure that every patient who leaves the building has another appointment. Their next hygiene appointment, a treatment, a follow up, a consult....something. Your staff needs to make sure the patient is coming back. As the patient leaves, be sure to thank them in a personalized manner. It is very important to say "Thank you". Saying "Have a great day" and typical things people say is fine but also thank them for their time and choosing your practice.

Spouse in the Practice

Most research shows that around 70% of spouses are employed by the smaller to medium dental practices. There are many of reasons to employ a spouse in the practice: retirement savings benefits, lower tax benefits and embezzlement prevention. The spouse not only helps with the family's bottom line, they can help keep a watchful eye on the practice while the dentist drills and fills. However, there seems to be a general unease among other staff when a small dental practice employs the spouse.

For some reason, the spouse is instantly disliked and disrespected when they are an employee. Many spouses that are practice employees are resented because they did not have to go through the hiring process and seem to be held at a different standard than other employees. Also, spouses tend to have special privileges (like leaving early, time off, etc.).

There are three ways to help the staff accept the spouse and understand their role in the operation of the office. First, the spouse is an extension of the business owner. He or she is typically partially responsible for the practice's success, debt, losses, gains and all business practices. He or she has taken on a lot of risk so it is natural for the spouse to participate at some level. If the spouse is more of a background player, he or she is still involved. The spouse usually has shared risk like the owner, whether it be debt, insurance and other liablities. Practices, no matter how they are legally set up, are still family businesses and the spouse has a voice in the practice. Many times just communicating how important it is to you, the business owner, to have your spouse's support will soften perception. If the staff sees that it is important to the owner, they will try to make things work.

Second, the spouse is normally employed as a business office professional and this is a bonus for the business office. This is a good thing because he or she can see the business office professionals shine and report how good they are at their positions. Typically the dentist has very little interaction with the business office on a day-to-day basis. So, the spouse can really give out the praise they deserve.

Third, if the spouse works in the business, he or she must have well-defined responsibilities so that he or she does not interfere with other duties in the business office. A loose approach to the spouse's duties just causes confusion and anger among employees. In fact, all jobs need to be defined and refined from time to time. It helps everyone perform better and know how to handle issues should they appear.

Lastly, the spouse should take their role seriously and keep certain hours. That way everyone will know when he/she is in the office and when they can count on their contribution to the practice.

Can't We All Just Get Along?

Many times offices face conflict among employees. It can get ugly and can linger. Facing employee issues might be the most difficult thing about running a practice or small business. On the other hand, it can be very rewarding to see everyone getting a long as a team.

It is incumbent upon the business owner to tell employees what he/she expects. For example, tell everyone that you expect them to resolve any conflicts before involving the business owner. They should not approach the business owner over issues unless all efforts have been exhausted. The business owner should not get involved unless it is affecting patients or overall morale.

The 1-2-3 Approach is an excellent method of helping employees deal with interpersonal issues.

One, how does the conflict affect the patient? Is the conflict helping patients or hindering their care? How can the issue be resolved in the best interest for the patient?

If it does not affect the patient then move on to Question Number Two: how does it affect the business? Is the conflict affecting the business? If so, how can the issue be

16

resolved for the best outcome for the practice/business? Is it helping or hindering the business?

If the business is not affected, then ask Question Number Three. How does the conflict effect the individual? That is where most conflicts arise; it is a personal issue.

However, if you back away from the issue and look at it from the patient first then the business second, many times you will find the answer there. If the issue truly is personal, each employee should express their perspective and work to find a common ground. If there is no common ground, the business owner may have to get involved to set up a new way to interact.

If your staff has issues with each other and you as the business owner have to get involved often because the staff cannot fix quarrels by themselves, then you need to take action with the problem employees. The employees who complain the most and involve the business owner most often in conflicts are the ones that usually are the first to lose their jobs. You will need to coach your staff to find a way to get along or you will find lower maintenance employees.

Other Conflicts

In small businesses/practices, all employees are often on the same level, without a deep organizational structure. So the business owner is the boss and all the employees report to the boss. Often that sets up competition and petty gossip. Gossip is death to a practice. Patients see it and it makes everyone uncomfortable. It does not seem to matter what age or gender, employees love to talk about each other. This goes back to our "hire slow" approach. Use your interviews and personality testing to avoid hiring employees with this trait. That way you weed out the serious Gossip before they poison the entire staff.

But what if you already have your staff in place? At your next staff meeting you must have a "preventative talk". Just like preventative medicine/dentistry, tell your staff you are advising them how to keep in good standing with their employer. Institute a "no gossip" policy and ask that they keep themselves in check at all times. Make sure all employees understand that the No Gossip policy extends to patients as well. The last thing you want to happen is staff talking about patients and other patients overhearing it. That's another easy way to lose a patient.

"Whose fault is it?" is always the first question asked when something goes wrong, and it should not be. You should ask, "How is this being solved?" Some conflicts are difficult to resolve because it seems that blaming others makes the blamer look good. The blamer does this so they look better in other's eyes and they talk about who is wrong rather than resolution. One of the most mature things I have ever seen in an office is a staff that accepts responsibility and other staff members forgive them. The staff member who says, "Oops. I made a mistake. Let me correct this mistake and I will follow up on the result." is a great employee.

This works because everyone makes mistakes so accept that and commend the staff member who accepts accountability

Everyone is going to make errors so how you handle them will affect how you are perceived. You need to set an example by not blaming others because that makes you look bad and when you make a mistake, your staff will quickly point it out and that begins a downward spiral of poor morale and backbiting. Take responsibility, forgive and move on. If all employees take this approach, then all employees will get along better.

Corporate Bully

There is a growing problem in offices all around the U.S. and that is corporate bullying. In large corporations there is zero tolerance for the office bully but in small businesses, this problem is rarely addressed. It is often brushed under the carpet and not talked about.

However, bullying occurs and the business owner needs to be aware of it and stop it as soon as it is seen in the workplace. Common incidents are verbal abuse, verbal intimidation, threats and general condescending behavior.

If an employee is intimidating or threatening another employee it is cause for termination. Many times the situation can be resolved with an official conversation. Document the conversation and place it in both employees' files. But if it does not stop immediately, you must be prepared to take action.

Management 101

Managing a group of staff members is more of a job than you probably were aware of when you started your practice. You must know how to zig when they zag and lead in the toughest of times.

What follows is a list of situations and solutions to refer to when staff management becomes a challenge. The steps mostly are centered around how you can help staff members focus their attitude and their activities to support the business. If you manage them well, it will run as smooth as silk. If you ignore the warning signs, you will lose control. The overall common theme to these suggestions is communication. Communicate how you feel often and always think about what is beneficial for the patient and practice.

There are policies and procedures your office follows to operate smoothly. So why not have a written procedure about how to handle conflict and how staff members interact? There needs to be an atmosphere of respect and staff "chemistry" established by the owner.

Order: Every decision, interaction and conflict has to follow a natural order. By following this "order," your best decisions, interactions and conflict resolutions will naturally be resolved. The "order" to remember is that the patient comes *first*, the practice comes *second* and the individual comes *third*. If you follow this order in everything, most problems and challenges will be easily resolved.

The patient comes first: Their treatment and fulfilling that treatment in a professional and efficient manner is the first rule of order. Always consider the best treatment and solution for the patient. When considering this first, you should be able to resolve the majority of all office issues. If a staff issue comes up that involves a patient then the staff member needs to resolve it by considering the patient first before their personal needs. If your issue is not patient-related, move on to the second rule.

The practice comes second: This is important when dealing with money, office polices and staff interactions. The practice must make a profit so the staff, the power bill and the business expenses can be paid; otherwise there is no business to treat the patients. This consideration should always be applied when collecting fees, filing insurance and making sound financial decisions. If you have staff members who do not get along or staff members not following the rules, them always ask them, "Is this what best serves the practice?" Petty conflict takes time, reduces revenue and eats into efficiency. Playing referee is not what the dentist should be doing day in and day out. The dentist should ask the staff how they would handle a conflict by weighing all the factors involved and how the outcome affects the practice.

The third and last part of our "order" is **the individual comes third**. The staff member needs help in scheduling their time, their pay/bonus and their responsibilities.

If there is a conflict and the first two rules of order do not resolve an issue, then consider the individual needs. All individual needs should be considered equally but the individual needs *never* outweigh the patient or practice. If a staff member is very self-centered and needs their way in the issue, perhaps you should consider hiring a replacement. Open communication about personal needs and how they affect the business needs to be documented and emphasized to the employees.

As long as we remember the order of **Patient – Practice – Individual**, priorities can be placed on every decision.

Trust: You should set an example of respecting other's opinions and trusting them. Laugh off criticism and show your staff that day-to-day petty things do not matter. Many offices make it a practice to laugh about small mistakes and make light of it. This is a good mode of operation.

Lightening up the atmosphere keeps everyone happier and this translates to the patient. The patient sees that everyone is happy so they feel more comfortable being treated at your friendly practice.

Atmosphere: There is always a certain chemistry in every office. More than likely you have created an office ambience that follows your personality. If you are moody, the practice is moody. If you are upbeat and friendly, so is your practice. Your practice mimics your personality.

Put yourself in your staff's shoes, are you a good leader and are you a good manager? Your staff probably has a great chemistry together and is great to the patients. Approach your day the way you want the mood in the office to be.

Friendly, approachable, open, happy and smart are all positive adjectives describing you and your office. Embody these words daily and you will create an atmosphere that delights the patients. Your staff members will be happy and will reflect a great atmosphere for your business.

All in all, if you follow an order to resolve issues, build trust in the office and personify a positive atmosphere, your practice will reflect a successful and less stressful business. You will be a trendsetter in management and it will be easier to manage staff and patient relationships.

Marketing

Marketing 101

Getting the word out about your great practice is fun and challenging at the same time. Every market is different so embrace the concepts that work for you. Always look at what others are doing around you and see if it is successful. Join a mastermind group and share marketing ideas with them.

Print advertisement is not being used as much as it has been in the past. However, the old fashioned "cold calling" still works. If you have a talented marketer on your staff, I recommend you send them out one day a week and knock on doors. Have him or her call on local businesses with an offer. Some markets offer a free second opinion, a free first visit or free whitening with their first check up. Whatever your offer, print up professional coupons and hit the road. Call on churches, apartments, businesses, other medical practices, specialists, etc. If you like to make calls as the owner, go for it! It will have a big impact.

Another way to attract new patients is to call on businesses that provide dental insurance to their employees and you are a provider of that insurance. Call the Human Resources department and let them know you are a provider and any benefits your practice provides their employees. In other words, what is in it for their employees? Find ways to attract these new patients with your phenomenal service, your on-time appointments, your years of service, your reviews and anything that makes your office special. You need to pinpoint what makes your office great and use that in all your promotional material. You can also offer to give a talk to their staff. Speaking about dentistry and how they can improve their health is beneficial to the HR department and will show good will on your part.

If you are not visible on internet search engines, get to it. Drop all your old marketing methods and sink your money into the internet because that is how people shop. Make sure you are involved in sites that provide active reviews because potential patients check reviews before they venture out to a healthcare provider.. Also, if you are in-network with dental/medical insurance companies, make sure your practice is listed on their sites.

Social media is very popular so make sure you have a professional page somewhere on a Social Media outlet. Facebook, LinkedIn, Google Plus and Twitter are all very useful. There are great consultants who concentrate on social media marketing so if you do not feel comfortable with social media, hire an expert and get noticed on line.

Track how you get patients. Your business office should be entering every patient into your dental/medical software with details about how the patient found you. Run a report every three months to see where you are getting your patients. Put your marketing dollars into the highest number of referrals.

Many times you will find that most of your new patients come from existing patients. You need to personally thank those patients for their referral. Send them a nice note and if your budget allows, send a reasonably priced gift or gift card. Some offices offer a referral program. "$50 towards your next visit if you refer a new patient to our practice" is a common reward program. Please check your state dental board to verify if a program like this is within the limits of law. For most states, it is fine to reward your patients but is not acceptable to reward other dental professionals.

Sales, The dirty word

Is "sales" a dirty word in a professional dental or medical office? No, it is not a bad word. Sales must happen to run a basic business. You can call it appointments, consults or any word you would like but it comes down to asking the customer for their business. Yes, you are serving the public but consider this, all businesses, if they are for profit, must make sales a priority.

Sales involves many steps but the most important step is closing the sale. The whole sales cycle is prospecting, presentation and closing. The prospect stage happens when the patient has an appointment. The patient is in the chair. The presentation is when you and your Hygienist or Assistant present a treatment to the patient. You outline the treatment, what is prescribed and how the treatment will take place. Then the patient is presented a monetary plan by the front. If the patient is convinced they need the treatment and it costs what they expect then they are "closed" with a new appointment for the treatment. This sales cycle can go very smoothly if the entire staff is working in tandem.

For an example, here is a typical "sales cycle" that I see in a dental office:

The case was presented and you did a great job showing Ms. Smith, your patient, the intraoral pictures and x-rays of tooth #14. Her tooth had a large 20-year-old amalgam that covered a cusp and it had an obvious crack. You and your hygienist convinced the patient that they needed a crown because the tooth might break and they would then be facing a root canal or an extraction. The patient then asks when she can come in and you direct her to the front desk to make her appointment.

"Great," you think. "I need that crown on my schedule to make my production goals this month." One hour later, you check the schedule only to find out the patient did not schedule.

"Why?" you think. "That was a slam-dunk."

You dash to the front desk and ask Cindy, your scheduler, "What happened to Ms Smith?"

Cindy replies, "Ms. Smith decided to wait. I don't think she can afford the crown. She runs a small business so I do not think she has the money."

She decided to wait. Really? Since when did the patient decide their treatment course? That tooth's days are numbered and Ms. Smith will be in pain soon. Why did Cindy decide Ms Smith could not afford it? How does she know how Ms. Smith manages her money? Cindy does not and should not make that assumption. Many patients care about their teeth and like to avoid pain so in reality, Cindy did not help Ms Smith; she actually hurt her.

This story explains how we lose sales on a day-to-day basis because one important team member did not do an adequate job supporting the business.

We think of "sales" as a dirty word but like it or not, without "sales" your practice will not survive. In this case, you did a great job selling but your staff did a bad job closing the sale. Your business office staff must be prepared to close every sale. This is one of the most important steps in sales...the close. Being prepared with the correct order of how to present the case and get the schedule full is the most significant lesson to learn about closing the sale. It is critical to your business.

First, your hygienist must take intraoral pictures to support the case and present the photos to your patient. When you examine the patient after the hygienist has completed her/his work (prophy, probing and xrays), you must support her or him in their findings (unless it is truly a poor diagnosis). Prospects (patients) must hear the "proposal/ treatment and benefit" three times in order to understand and buy into the sale. The hygienist and the dentist are the first two steps. Your business office is the last step and closing step.

Your business office must be organized so that the best "salesperson" is the staff member who checks out all patients. Following a specific outline on how to close the sale will assist your "salesperson/closer" with filling the schedule.

Cindy the scheduler now becomes the scheduler/closer. She needs to help the patient with all the business side of her treatment. If Cindy had followed these steps, she would have been successful in closing Ms. Smith.

Your closing outline is:

Transition to Scheduler/closer: When the hygienist brings the patient to the business office, the scheduler/closer greets the patient and listens to the diagnosis from the hygienist.

Emphasize treatment: Once hearing the diagnosis, the scheduler/closer says, "Wow. We need to take care of you right away. It sounds like you need a crown due to the crack and large amalgam on that upper molar. I had a patient the other day who let it go only one week and now they are facing a root canal." It is important to verify that they need the work, tell them you will take care of *them* (not a thing or issue, you want to make this personal) and help them get the treatment completed.

Schedule the appointment: The scheduler/closer gets the appointment scheduled next. This is critical before any financial arrangements are presented. The appointment step is the first thing you do to close the sale. The scheduler/closer says something like, "Well, let's get you on the schedule. What is a good day for you Ms. Smith?" Get the appointment scheduled rather than talking about the cost. The treatment must be the focus of the closing conversation.

Financial arrangements: After the appointment is scheduled, the scheduler/closer asks the patient if they need to go over the fees. "Ms. Smith, would you like for me to go over your portion after insurance?" The patient will then talk about this if they want. Some do not care so just place a note in their chart that the patient did not care to discuss financial arrangements. However, most of the time, the patient very much cares about payment so give them ample time to discuss this very important part of the closing.

Note: When discussing money, the scheduler/closer must be sensitive to who is standing nearby or can overhear. I suggest you have a private place to talk to a patient and if it is a big case, then ask the patient to join you in a conference room. Make privacy a priority on sensitive topics.

Let's suppose Ms. Smith does not have the money up front to pay her portion of the crown. Your scheduler/closer cannot fumble this play. They can be empathetic but they should not let the patient whine about it. Your scheduler/closer must keep the patient focused on what treatment needs to be done rather than the overall economy or the patient's personal finances. If the scheduler gets caught up in the "woe is me" conversation, then the patient will not make the appointment or worse, will cancel later.

The scheduler/closer should focus the patient back to the treatment by saying something like, "Yes, Ms. Smith, times are tough for some. Now, back to your crown. I am very concerned about your health. Let's figure out how we can help you get the treatment you need while balancing the costs. We do not want you to go untreated. We can work something out. Let's try...." Assume they have the ability to pay and get them on the calendar. Again, do not get caught up in any negative conversation about cash, keep the patient focused on their treatment and why it is important.

Sometimes your scheduler/closer must get creative to work out the financial arrangements. There are so many great payment options available now such as Care-Credit and Springstone. That is the first option in helping patients with money. Also, monthly credit card billing is an option. This is for your long-term patients and not for new patients. Get creative on how to help the patient pay for their portion. Some crown patients pay half at prep and half at seat. If you make your own crowns, then you can have the patient pay half at the appointment and half in 30 days. (Just have a way to remind your staff to collect the balance.) Sometimes you have to get creative with financing and do not focus on costs too early in the closing part of the sale.

Dismiss the patient: Last, tell the patient when the practice will see her to help her with her treatment. "Ms. Smith, we look forward to seeing you on the 18th at 2:00. We will take very good care of you." is a good way to finalize your agreement to schedule the treatment and you know the sale is closed. Once the patient leaves the office, document how the payment will be handled and place the information in the appointment note section so if another business office person checks out the patient at appointment time, they will know what to collect.

Once you've gone through this training, you can present cases to patients with confidence because your scheduler/ closer will now be armed with a plan to fill your schedule. Remember it takes three conversations to convince a prospect/patient to understand the treatment and benefit. Make sure your staff is on board on how to close, so the patient gets the treatment they deserve.

Collections

Collections are a difficult part of running a business for employees as well as the patient. Treating patients with respect is the priority when collecting a debt.

Has your staff ever talked to a patient about their treatment and they were very clear about the patient's financial responsibility only to find out when the time comes to collect the fee, the patient gets "convenience amnesia"? This convenience amnesia is a problem if the patient uses this as an excuse to not pay their invoice. This is when you have to be creative and think on your feet.

It is often helpful to revisit the initial quote for the work performed. The conversation could go like this: "Ms. Smith, I am glad you received your treatment today. It sounds like it was a successful appointment. As you might remember when we set up your appointment, you and I had an agreement as to what your estimated payment would be. It sounds like you may be thinking something different." Then listen to what she says and work with her from there.

Sometimes, patients want the treatment and they have a spouse or friend convince them that they do not have to pay the full amount or that they should delay payment.

The patient presents a new plan when it is time to check out and pay the bill. This is frustrating for the staff so for cases like this, you need a stiff office policy on how to handle the change. The policy needs to be to collect some part of the invoice and have a written commitment from the patient about their future responsibility. Your staff will need something in writing in case the patient has to be turned over to a collection agency. Tell your staff to collect something and if they need to, put the patient on a payment plan. Put it in writing.

All staff should focus on all patients settling all balances when they check out

Unscheduled Treatment Plans – The Low-Hanging Fruit.

"The low-hanging fruit" is a term that salespeople use and it refers to the easy sale point. Salespeople always know which client to go to when they need to boost sales or have a product that can be sold quickly. The medical dental office makes "sales" from small incremental treatments so there is really no product or service that specifically can be considered as a quick sale to boost production. Therefore, you have no set of patients to go to for "low hanging fruit."

However, you do have the unscheduled treatment plan list available; this is your low hanging fruit. Print out your unscheduled list from the prior six months. Your staff should start calling this list the day it is printed and continue until the list is exhausted. Most dental and medical software provides you with a way to print this very important report.

Print the list every month and include all unscheduled treatment from six months before. This list is helpful in two ways. One, it can help you clean up any treatment that has been posted already or needs to be updated or deleted. Second, it gives you a "call list" because it is treatment that is necessary but for whatever the reason, the patient has not scheduled.

Check each line item for details before calling the patient. The details you need to check include the patient's current balance. Are they a bad payer, no payer or slow payer? Leave these patients to the last ones to call; still call them but just do not make them your priority. Then check the treatment notes and any other notes about the specific treatment. That way you will have the information you need to assist the patient with their questions about their treatment.

Here is an example of what your staff can say when you call: "Hi Ms. Smith, this is Mary with Big Time Dentistry. Dr. Martin and I were going through charts today and we noticed you have not scheduled your composite filling yet. He is concerned about your tooth because there is active decay. So, as a courtesy, I wanted to call you to remind you to schedule your treatment as soon as possible." Then stop talking and see what they say. No pressure, no big words, no argument...make it very comfortable for the patient to make a decision on their own. Either schedule the appointment or document what was said into the chart so you have a record of the conversation.

Typically the unscheduled treatment plan is a large report especially if you include everything that was diagnosed in the last year. Sometimes it can be overwhelming to start calling patients from this list because it is so long. It looks like you will never finish. Reassure your staff that calling a certain amount every day will keep them on track. Set goals of how many calls will be made and how many contacts will be made either by leaving a voice mail or voice to voice contact. It might be a good idea to hire a part time employee who is great at sales to take on this task so it frees up the business office staff. It would more than pay for itself if they can get a couple of appointments scheduled per hour. This one task can have a huge impact on filling your schedule.

When your business office staff member sits down to perform this task, they should have three things in mind: One, take this task seriously, two, have a goal of a certain number of calls to make at each sitting and three, have a monetary goal of how much production is scheduled for the week. Making at least 10 calls per sitting and a weekly monetary goal of $5,000 production should be the goal. I also recommend a bonus for this staff member if they book over $25,000 per month. You will need to set a schedule coding system to track how the appointment was booked. The patient has to have the treatment and pay for the treatment before the bonus is paid. Trust me, the staff member will keep up with this but you will need to have them provide you reports so you can track it.

Another unscheduled treatment plan your staff needs to print and work with is the daily report. All your staff needs to do is to print the unscheduled treatment dated for the next week. For example, if today is Tuesday, March 7 print next Tuesday, March 14's unscheduled treatment plan. Scan the schedule with the patients who have unscheduled treatment. See if their appointment coincides with an opening in the operative department's schedule right before or right after their hygiene. (I am assuming the patient is coming in for a hygiene appointment but you should run the same report for operative patients with continuing care so that you can place patients into the hygiene schedule as well.) Check all notes, charting and ledger information. Then call the patient to get them on the schedule.

The business office professional calls the patient and says something like, "Hi Ms. Smith, This is Mary with Awesome Dentistry. I think you already know you are scheduled a week from today to see Becky for your hygiene appointment. When Becky and I were reviewing your chart this morning, we saw that you have not scheduled that crown yet. I know your time is valuable so we thought we would call you as a courtesy to see if you wanted to save time to go ahead and take care of this while you are here next week." Then stop talking and see what they say. The fact that the patient needs work and they are already planning to be here is a good motivator for the patient to schedule. You might only get one per day but it is worth your time to call these patients.

Now, here is an idea to combine the unscheduled treatment calls with the duties of the spouse. I have found that this task is a great task for the spouse. The spouse is highly motivated to bring business in. She/he feels the same pressure as the business owner to pay the bills. Also, the spouse has a good direct line to the dentist so they can get treatment information fast prior to calling the patient. The dentist is more apt to spend time with the spouse explaining procedures. This gives the spouse a great deal of extra information so they can close the sale.

My Biggest Concern

Closing the sale/treatment schedule is very important to the profitability of the practice. The strongest production offices have a good closer in the business office. However, you need to make sure everyone who talks to patients about scheduling their treatment is trained on one simple concept, "My biggest concern is...". This is an old sales technique that really works great in the dental and medical business.

The business office professional needs to be prepared to discuss their issues with closing the sale/treatment. Here is a good example of how the conversation may occur: "Ms. Smith now that we have your appointment scheduled, I have a concern. My biggest concern is that insurance does not pay what I am anticipating. Sometimes insurance does not pay exactly what they promise so I am concerned that we will have a problem with what we have estimated to be your portion." Then stop talking.

This gives the patient a chance to discuss your concern and understand that there may be an issue with their insurance portion, their past history of broken appointments, their possible root canal after taking out a massive amount of decay, etc. This technique is great for the clinical staff to use also. For example, "Ms. Smith, I have a concern. Your periodontal pockets are getting deeper and my biggest concern is that someday you will lose your teeth and if we do not address this soon, you will start to see long term problems such as tooth loss." Then stop and see what the patient says. This is a great way to express the importance of their treatment and your trained clinical opinion.

The Word "Yet"

When closing a sale/treatment or even when the clinical staff talks to a patient a sense of urgency should be used when appropriate. Use the word "yet" when talking with patients. "Does it hurt yet? Are you in pain yet?" really emphasizes to patients that you are trying to prevent any new problems from occurring. It is your job to help patients understand that postponing treatment does not make it go away. Teeth and gums do not heal without help. There are no medicines that can make the condition change. Using the word "yet" often helps patients understand what is going on with their oral health and know there are repercussions of doing nothing.

You can't fail prospecting unless you fail to prospect

You should always make it a priority to find new business. Yes, your existing patient base will be the majority of your production for the coming year but you always need new patients. Prospecting is very important particularly if you are a specialist.

Specialists need to take general dentists to lunch, send treats to the general dentist's staff and conduct Lunch & Learns with dentists. If you can work with your state dental board in designing a continuing education course, then set up a great course that makes you known as the expert in the field. This will get staff and dentists referring to you.

If you are a general dentist, conduct a class for your patients and ask them to bring a friend. The class can be about anything you are interested in. Offer discounts if they make an appointment that day and offer giveaways to get people in. Timing is everything so plan the day and time of the week carefully. Send an email to all patients and specialists about the class. Having new patients referred from the specialist is a home run.

Also, visit apartments, real estate companies that represent large residential groups, retirement villages and medical businesses close by. Your goal is to do two calls a week.

Another way to prospect is to have a staff member call on businesses around your office and invite them in for a free consult or free second opinion. Make up professional cards or brochures stating your offer. If you get a new patient in asking for a second opinion, often you will be their dentist of choice. The last dentist the patient talks with will usually be the one they make an appointment with.

Miscellaneous

Exclamation marks!

When documenting the patient's treatment or anything with regards to patient written correspondence, please do not use exclamation marks! Everything is not amazing! Everything is not that important! When you read exclamations in sentences, it seems like you are yelling! Please refrain from this unprofessional writing! Please!

Stand While Talking

When you are presenting a treatment plan, you should stand to show authority. The clinical person should stand while presenting or sit very upright and tall. Typically the patient is in the chair and looking up at you anyway so standing is not an issue. If you are both in the consult room, then stand and seat the patient. Stand while presenting and use the computer screen to present X-rays and intra oral pictures. When the patient is transitioned to the business office, the business office staff should stand while setting an appointment. Sometimes this is difficult because most offices are configured to have the staff member seated and the patient on the other side of the desk standing. The patient will probably always be standing so the staff member has to train themselves to stand once they have the appointment card and/or payment information to present. This shows respect and authority. Make sure you stand every time you present anything.

Insurance

Is being an in-network dental/medical insurance provider necessary to support your business? Insurance is the 800 lb. gorilla in the room; you just can't avoid it. You probably take many plans and hate dealing with all the write offs necessary to be in-network. The best way to approach insurance is to only accept plans that pay close to 83-85% of your rate or better. There are great consulting services to which you can pay a fee and they will negotiate rates for you. This is a great way to delegate that task because these consultants have more leverage than a sole practitioner can have when negotiating fees. Plus the consultant can run reports about the area's typical fees and assist you with that. If you do not want to pay a consultant, try to negotiate rates yourself. Only choose companies that pay your top codes in an acceptable manner. For example, if your practice is hygiene heavy in production, then negotiate those codes more heavily. You need to be in the 85% or better range of reimbursement of your top 10 codes.

Once you have decided what companies to be in-network with, then it is down to the basic day-to-day operation of managing the payment and the patient's expectations. Dental insurance is different than medical insurance. Many times your staff has to explain to the patients that their dental insurance typically only covers a percentage of their procedures. Your staff needs to spend time with patients training them how their insurance works.

Your staff needs a good working knowledge of insurance and must communicate the insurance percentages to the patients. Being exact on the patient portion is very difficult, but crucial to patient satisfaction. I recommend you give them a "Good Faith Estimate" rather than a patient responsibility amount. The staff must explain that insurance is the patient's responsibility and we can only interpret what the insurance company tells the practice.

Have your staff say the word, "Estimate" 5000 times a day and you should be safe. Also, please have all patients sign a responsibility form. The form can be found in your dental software documents to download for each patient. If you do not have it with your software, you can easily find online forms from many dental websites. It is good to explain to the patient that dental insurance does not typically cover 100% of dental needs so your practice collects at the time of service unless the patient makes prior arrangements. Forms are important because if you ever end up in a battle with a patient, it is a good idea to have documentation for your reference.

Wrapping Up The 3 M's

Running a dental and medical office is fun yet difficult. If you apply the 3 M's - Management, Marketing and Miscellaneous, you will have no choice but to be successful. I hope these tips and ideas have inspired you to deal with work and work the deal. I commend you for reading about making your business a success. It is important to enjoy your day and implement a few new ideas. You never know, one idea might change your business forever.

And remember:

Approach your day positively. Give positive feedback and you will receive back positive feedback.

About the Author

Maryann Bateman is a dental practice administrator in Charlotte, NC. She has a BA in Business Administration and Fine Art from The University of North Carolina at Chapel Hill and a BA in Architecture from UNCC College of Architecture. Maryann is a graduate of Sandler Sales Institute/Dunn Training, the ISSA Fitness Nutrition Specialist Certification Program and the Health Coaching Certification program from The Institute of Integrative Nutrition in New York City, NY. Maryann has written several articles that can be found on-line at dentistryiq.com.

Made in the USA
Monee, IL
15 September 2023

42833631R10036